Fox and Cubs

By Carmel Reilly

Yez the fox sits in her den.

Her six cubs are
at the den, too.

The cubs get fed. Yum!

It is hot.

Yez zips up to the dam.

Yez and the six cubs go for a dip.

The cubs get wet!

Yez can see men at the dam.

The fox cubs see
the men, too.

Yez and the cubs run.

Yez and the cubs
zip into the den.

Yip! Yip!

Yez and the cubs nap.

CHECKING FOR MEANING

1. How many cubs does Yez the fox have? *(Literal)*

2. Where do Yez and her cubs go when it is hot? *(Literal)*

3. Why did Yez and her cubs go back to the den? *(Inferential)*

EXTENDING VOCABULARY

fox	What are some words you could use to describe a fox? Is it fast or slow? Is it big or small? Does it feel rough or smooth?
Yum	What is the meaning of *yum* in this text? What is another word that has a similar meaning? Can you use it in a sentence?
zip	What does *zip* mean in this text? What else can *zip* mean?

MOVING BEYOND THE TEXT

1. When you are feeling hot, what can you do to cool off?

2. Where does a fox have its den? Why?

3. What food do cubs have? Where do they get it from?

4. What do mother foxes teach their cubs so they can learn to live on their own?

SPEED SOUNDS

Xx	Yy	Zz				
Kk	Ll	Vv	Qq	Ww		
Dd	Jj	Oo	Gg	Uu		
Cc	Bb	Rr	Ee	Ff	Hh	Nn
Mm	Ss	Aa	Pp	Ii	Tt	

PRACTICE WORDS

fox

Yez

six

zips

Yum

zip

Yip